GUITAR HARMONY

FOR THE
ROCK GUITARIST

BY DAVID BREWSTER

ISBN 978-1-57424-346-8
SAN 683-8022

D'Angelico Excel SS Model Guitars on the front and back cover.

Cover by James Creative Group

Copyright © 2017 CENTERSTREAM Publishing, LLC
P.O. Box 17878 - Anaheim Hills, CA 92817

www.centerstream-usa.com | centerstrm@aol.com

David Brewster is an honors graduate from the Atlanta Institute of Music, and has several books published by Hal Leonard, Centerstream Publications, and Cherry Lane. He's also a writer and contributor for Guitar Player and Premier Guitar magazine.

In addition to his educational background and published works, he's taught guitar and music for over 20 years, including teaching for Guitar Center Studios, The National Guitar Workshop, School of Rock, and at colleges and universities across the Midwest.

His performance background includes touring and recording with several national acts, and David has independently released several instrumental guitar albums, including music tributes to Edgar Allan Poe, HR Giger, and HP Lovecraft.

For more information about David, visit his Soundcloud profile at www.soundcloud.com/david-brewster

Special thanks go to Courtney Simon, who helped me edit and save this book! We're soulmates and you've stolen my heart. Thanks babe! XOXO

Contents

Introduction

Welcome to the world of harmonized guitar playing and music! This book will locate, define, and reveal some of the mysteries behind building harmonized guitar parts, and by working through these concepts and ideas, you'll gain insight into using a variety of harmonization techniques, while simultaneously becoming exposed to the layout and construction of intervals in music. Intervals are the measured distance between two (or more) notes sounded in music, and studying them will improve your ear immensely, not to mention help you understand scales and modes, chord construction, and how you can add harmonized and intervallic ideas into your music.

As you progress through this book, you'll be exposed to building 2, 3, and 4-part harmony using a series of exercises and harmonized phrases. If you don't have a second guitarist that can harmonize and play these examples along with you, you can always use a loop pedal, record the harmonized phrases separately, or play along with the accompanying audio examples, mainly so you can experience what performing harmonized music feels like for yourself.

You should notice that the majority of this book involves taking a scale or melodic phrase, and cycles it through a series of different harmonized approaches, incorporating harmonized notes from above and below, which produces different results. Doing this type of side-by-side comparison will help you see (and hear) the variety of harmonized options available to you, which will lead to additional experiments and discoveries for you in the future.

The ideas shown and presented in this guide can be related or incorporated into any style of music, but for our purposes here, the overall style will center around rock guitar. While you can easily find harmonized ideas in other styles of music, harmonized guitar concepts and ideas have flourished in rock and metal music for decades, and because of this we'll focus our attention toward the most common harmonized ideas and sounds that rock and metal guitarists have been refining for years.

Good luck and have fun!

The History of Harmonized Guitar Music

The practice of building and recording guitar harmonies is common for rock guitarists, and became popular when harmony parts appeared in popular music during the 1950's. One of the earliest innovators of layering electric guitar harmonies on recordings was the immortal Les Paul, who not only introduced the world to the electric guitar and multi-track recording during the 1940's and 1950's, he also crafted a pioneering style of layering and recording multiple guitar parts together, which helped him create an "orchestra" of multiple parts in his music, and influenced millions of people in the process.

Les Paul

Taking most of their ideas directly from Les, early rock artists continued to refine his layered recording techniques and further popularized these sounds during the 1950's and 1960's. The Beatles song 'And Your Bird Can Sing' features several sections featuring layered guitar tracks performing in harmony together. This song in particular inspired and influenced many guitarists to further investigate the world of harmonized guitar parts, and led to further experiments of creating harmonized ideas and recording techniques.

During the late 1960's, there were several companies that produced octave-based effect pedals, and guitar legend Jimi Hendrix was well-known for using an Octavia pedal in his rig, which helped him create the fuzzy octave tones heard in a number of his famous songs, including his seminal classic 'Purple Haze.' The use of this pedal and the interesting sounds it produced in Hendrix's music inspired numerous guitarists to experiment with octave effects for themselves, and helped push octave and harmony effects into the mainstream.

Harmonized guitar playing during the 1970's is widely considered its heyday, and you'll find countless examples of inspired harmonized guitar parts within this popular decade of music. If you listen carefully, you'll hear dual guitars distinctly featured in many popular songs, including classic hits from artists such as Queen, The Allman Brothers Band, Led Zeppelin, The Eagles, Boston, and Kiss. While harmonized guitars can be found in music before the 1970's, there's no denying that several inspired pioneers of harmonized guitar music really flourished during this decade of rock.

Iron Maiden

In the decades that followed, guitarists continued to push harmonized ideas and concepts further, and a number of songs from the 1980's and 1990's prominently feature harmony guitar parts. Groups and artists such as Iron Maiden, Metallica, Steve Vai, Yngwie Malmsteen, and Soundgarden continued the tradition of harmonized guitar playing, each creating a number of memorable harmonized guitar moments. Technology during these decades produced a number of popular effect pedals and rack-mounted units that produce harmonized sounds and effects, including big-sellers from companies such as Eventide, Digitech, and Boss. The products allow guitarists to select specific harmonized pitches and effects, which radically changed the sonic and compositional soundscape for guitarists, all over the world.

The practice of writing, recording, and performing harmonized guitar music continues today, and can be heard coming from guitarists and groups such as Animals As Leaders, Lamb of God, Periphery, and Muse. Guitar tones, playing techniques, and instrument designs have changed radically over the years, but the process of building harmonized parts remains the same, with noticeably more guitarists incorporating harmony than ever before.

Chapter 1 – Intervals and Basic Harmonization

The first step in understanding what harmonies are and how to produce your own harmonized ideas, would be learning as much as you can about intervals. An interval refers to the distance between two (or more) single-notes, and this refers to the distance between two notes of a scale, chord, arpeggio, or any arrangement of notes in music.

Each interval has a specific sound and a specific name, which is given for general identification and association. Within each octave of music, there are twelve interval names to become familiar with and memorize. An octave is the interval name given to two notes that have the same note name, but are distanced twelve half-steps apart. A half-step on the guitar is the distance between two notes that are one fret away from each other. For example, the distance between the notes C and C# on the third and fourth fret on the 'A' string is one half-step.

The easiest way to become familiar with intervals and the distance between them, is to examine and study their arrangement on a single string. Seeing and performing intervals in this manner will reveal the actual distance between each interval, along with supplying you with the basic sound and overall structure. Play through the first example, demonstrating the breakdown of intervals within a single octave, performed entirely on the 'A' string (Ex.1).

Ex.1 - Arrangement of Intervals

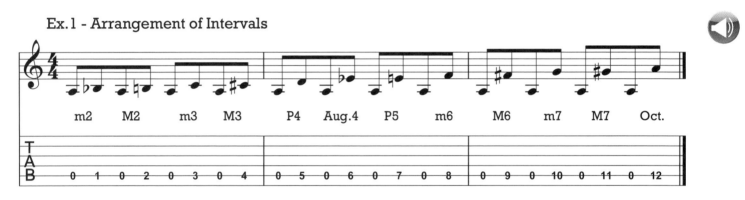

As you play through Ex.1, be sure that you listen carefully to how each two-note group sounds when played in order. Every interval has a specific sound and character, and while some of these intervals sound good to the ear (known as consonant intervals), others might sound bad to the ear (known as dissonant intervals). In the beginning, it would be wise to focus on learning how to use consonant intervals first. Once you become comfortable using simple harmonized approaches, then you can explore the unusual sounds and more challenging task of harmonizing dissonant intervals.

Another way of performing the same arrangement of intervals on the guitar is shown in the next example (Ex.2), where the layout of intervals are arranged across the bottom three strings of the guitar and in a single position, as opposed to the single-string method used in the previous example.

Ex.2 - Alternate Fingering of Ex.1

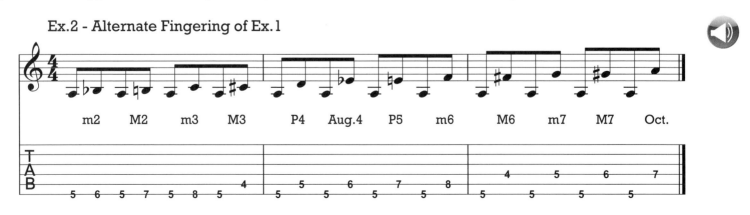

Now that you have a basic idea of what intervals are and how to find them on the fretboard, we should identify each interval by classifying them with a specific name for reference and study. The following chart should help you see the arrangement of intervals, along with the names of each and the specific order of intervals, from the starting note A to the final note A, one octave (12-notes) higher (Fig.1).

Be aware that the interval names and distance between the notes is universal in any key, so the actual note names would change if you were to apply this idea to another key. For our purposes here, we are defining intervals with the starting note A, but if you were to change to another note, the order of the interval names listed here (Minor 2nd to Perfect Octave) would remain the same, but the individual notes for each interval would change, and correspond with the new starting note. You should think of this arrangement of intervals and their names as a template that can easily be moved into other keys.

A to A#/Bb - Minor 2nd
A to B - Major 2nd
A to C - Minor 3rd
A to C#/Db - Major 3rd
A to D - Perfect 4th
A to D#/Eb - Augmented 4th/Flatted Fifth
A to E - Perfect 5th
A to F - Minor 6th
A to F#/Gb - Major 6th
A to G - Minor 7th
A to G#/Ab - Major 7th
A to A - Perfect Octave

Fig. 1

Harmonizing Consonant Intervals

Throughout this book, we'll mainly be examining and creating harmonized guitar parts using consonant intervals – which includes the Minor 3rd, Major 3rd, Perfect 4th, Perfect 5th, and Perfect Octave (Ex.3).

Ex.3 - Consonant Intervals

As you progress, other harmonized intervals will be introduced (such as 6ths), but the majority of these ideas will revolve around using and harmonizing consonant intervals. The reason for this centers on the fact that consonant intervals are pleasing to the ear, are relatively easy to harmonize, and are the most common harmonized sound heard in music.

While the vast majority of popular songs feature harmonized guitar parts using consonant intervals, it's highly recommended to explore and experiment with the unusual world of harmonizing dissonant intervals. The results of harmonizing dissonant intervals may shock your ears, but they're an interesting alternative to the sound of harmonized consonant intervals.

The next example demonstrates two guitars harmonized together, giving you the first look into two-part guitar harmonization, while also showcasing the arrangement of consonant intervals in the key of A (Ex.4).

Ex.4 - Harmonized Consonant Intervals

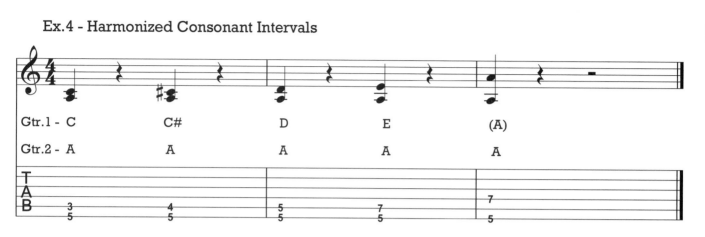

In the previous example (Ex.4), you should notice that Guitar 1 is performing a moving series of notes along the A string, sounding the notes C-C#-D-E-A. Guitar 2 stays on the root note (A) as the example moves along, revealing not only the combined sound of each interval written with the guitars performing together, but this also provides a basic example of creating harmony between the two guitars. The first guitar is sounding a series of notes (a melody part), while the second guitar counterbalances the first part, providing and creating the harmonization (a harmony part). This is a common method for basic two-part harmonization, but many other styles and methods will be explored and shown in this book.

To help you dive deeper into this manner of playing, you should learn how to harmonize a very common scale used in all forms of music, the Natural Minor Scale (a.k.a Aeolian), which is written here in the key of A Minor (Ex.5).

Ex.5 - A Natural Minor Scale (One Octave)

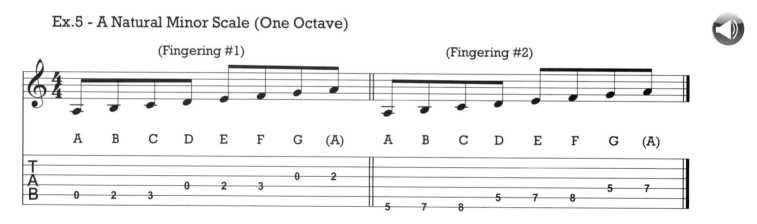

Parallel Harmonization

Before diving into the next example, a harmonized A Natural Minor scale, you should become aware of a concept and term known as parallel harmonization. Parallel harmonization occurs when a series of harmonized notes follow each other using a strict intervallic distance. In other words, a harmonized part that is limited to a specific interval - such as Parallel 4th's or 5th's.

To get a better understanding of performing parts parallel harmony, play through the next example, which features A Aeolian written using Parallel 3rds (Ex.6).

Ex. 6 - Harmonized A Nat. Minor Scale (Using Parallel 3rds)

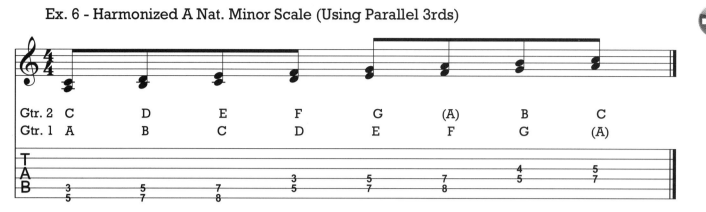

Listen to the audio carefully to reveal how the parallel harmonization technique sounds when performed together. The bottom line of notes (Gtr.1) performs the notes from A Aeolian, while the top line of notes (Gtr.2) follows the first guitar part, performed a third above.

Through the study of the intervallic distance between each of the notes in the previous example (Ex.6), it's revealed that the intervals contained are a combination of Minor and Major 3rds. The distance between the two parts never deviate from the interval distance of a third, thereby revealing a series of parallel thirds. Parallel harmonization can incorporate other consonant intervals, including 4ths, 5ths, and octaves. In traditional music theory, the use of Parallel 4ths, 5ths, and octaves is frowned upon and is considered theoretically wrong, but countless guitarists have utilized this type of harmonization and found the right ways to use it.

The next example demonstrates a variation of the previous example, but this time the second guitar part is performing notes from A Aeolian using Parallel 4ths (Ex.7).

Ex.7 - Harmonized A Nat. Minor Scale (Using Parallel 4ths)

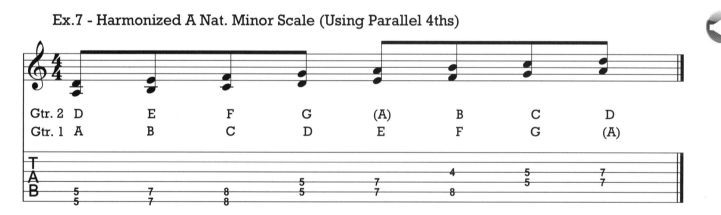

For the sake of comparison, examine and play through the next example, demonstrating A Aeolian harmonized using Parallel 5ths (Ex.8).

Ex.8 - Harmonized A Nat. Minor Scale (Using Parallel 5ths)

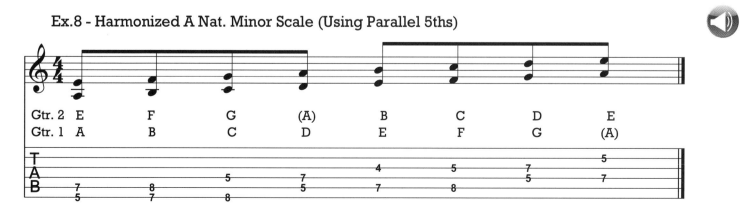

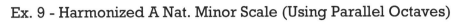

The next example demonstrates the same idea, but now we're incorporating Parallel Octaves (Ex.9).

Ex. 9 - Harmonized A Nat. Minor Scale (Using Parallel Octaves)

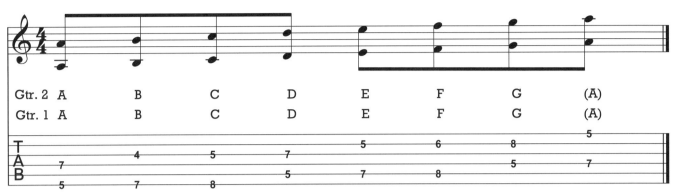

Once you have a grasp on the concept of locating and performing using the parallel harmonization approach, you should discover ways to harmonize a two-octave version of this scale. The following example is a common two-octave fingering for A Aeolian (Ex.10).

Ex.10 - Two-octave A Natural Minor Scale

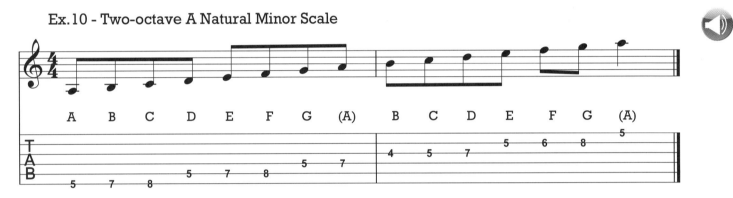

Now that you have the two octave fingering of A Aeolian under your fingers, play through the next example, demonstrating a harmonized two-octave version using Parallel 3rds (Ex.11).

Ex.11 - Harmonized Two-octave A Nat. Minor Scale (Using Parallel 3rds)

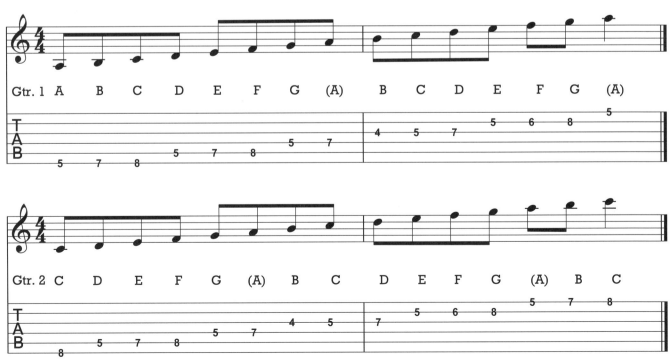

You should notice that the previous example recycles the scale fingering used in Ex.10, allowing you to perform a two-octave harmony within the same fretboard position. This single-position method of harmonization is quite common, and might require some experimentation as your harmony building skills improve.

The next example is a fingering and fretboard variation (or relocation) of the scale. Learning this position and comparing it with the previous example will allow expansion within the harmonization options available to you, and allow you to experiment with building harmonies using a different range of notes (Ex.12).

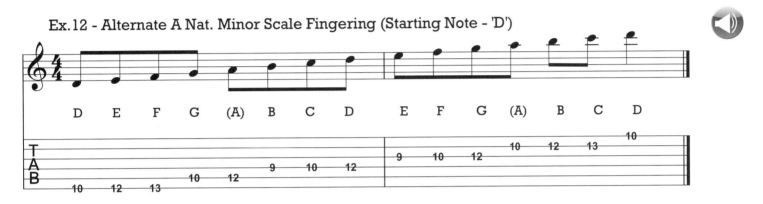

Now that you have a new scale fingering under your fingers, you should combine the new scale position with the original scale position shown in Ex.10, allowing you to create a harmonized A Aeolian using Parallel 4ths (Ex.13).

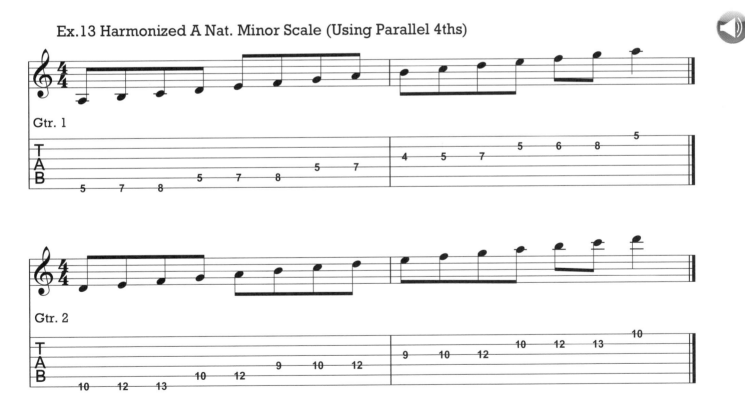

The next example shows the next position, which begins on the note E and is found at the 12th fret on the low E string (Ex.14).

Ex.14 - Alternate A Nat. Minor Scale Fingering (Starting Note - E)

Once the new fingering and position has been learned, you can begin harmonizing using Parallel 5ths, as shown in the next example (Ex.15).

Ex.15 - Harmonized A Nat. Minor Scale (Using Parallel 5ths)

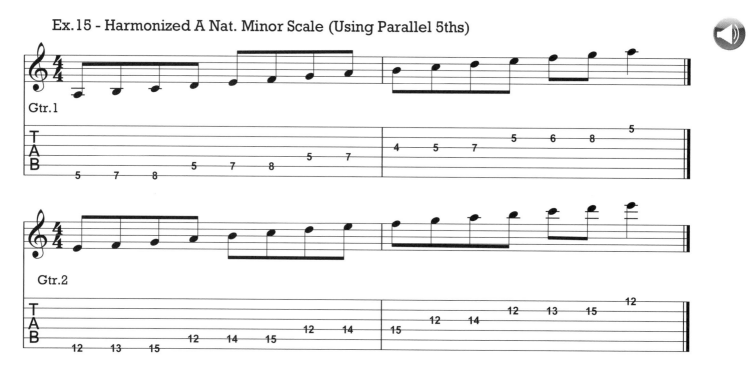

Now that you've explored harmonizing A Aeolian using Parallel 3rds, 4ths, and 5ths, you should practice the fingering presented in the next example, which is the mirror-image of Ex.10, a root-position fingering written one octave higher than where we started (Ex.16).

Ex.16 - A Nat. Minor Scale (One Octave Higher Than Ex.10)

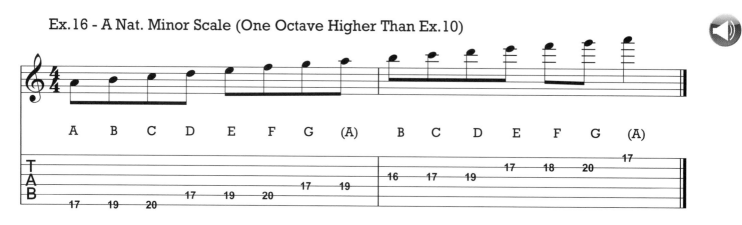

With the previous example under your fingers, practice the next example, a Parallel Octave version of A Aeolian (Ex.17).

Ex.17 - Harmonized A Nat. Minor Scale (Using Parallel Octaves)

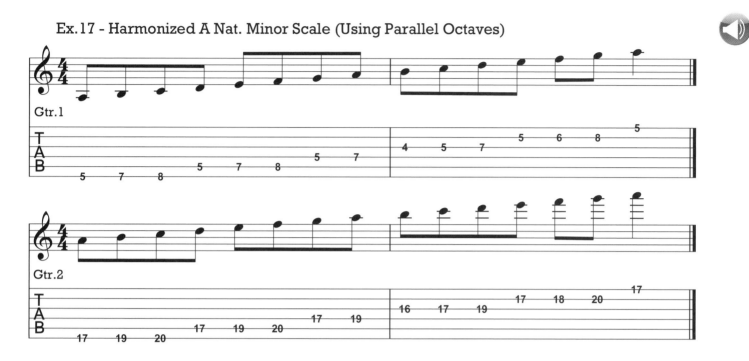

In this chapter you've navigated through a variety of approaches with harmonizing the A Natural Minor scale. The next step would be applying this information to other keys, which will expand these ideas to new sounds and directions. After you've played through these harmonized scales, you should write a few basic harmonized licks and phrases, so you can begin creating your own musical ideas. Although you can literally spend years studying harmonization concepts and techniques, the best way to really absorb them into your playing and into your music is through direct application and plenty of creative experimentation.

Lynyrd Skynyrd

Chapter 2 – Two-Part Harmony Using Minor Pentatonic Scales

Pentatonic scales are the most common scale that guitarists use in all forms of music, so it only makes sense that we should explore harmonizing this scale. We can use a combination of the basic scale harmonization techniques that were presented in the previous chapter, and through applying this information through a series of sample licks and phrases, we can reveal a variety of applied harmonization.

To begin, play through the next example, arguably the most common scale that guitarists perform and use in every style and genre of music, the A Minor Pentatonic scale located in the 5th position (Ex.18).

Ex.18 - A Minor Pentatonic Scale (Starting Note - A)

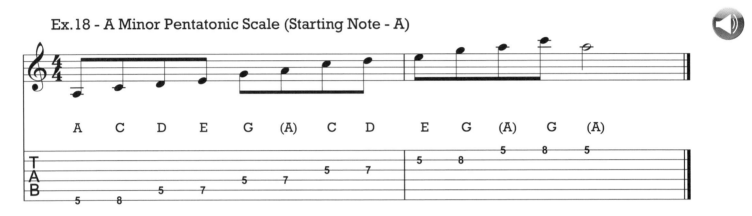

If you examine the notes contained within this scale, you should notice that all of the notes compared to the A Nat. Minor scale are found within its basic framework, with the exception of two notes. The 2nd and the 6th are removed from the Nat. Minor scale, creating the familiar five-note Pentatonic sound and two-note per-string scale fingering. In the key of A Minor, the removed 2nd and 6th intervals are the notes B and F, specifically.

Before we explore harmonizing this scale, it would be wise and useful to expand this scale into the next fretboard position. The following example demonstrates the next position of A Minor Pentatonic, which begins on the note C, a Minor 3rd away from the first note of the previous scale position (Ex.19), which is perfect to explore a basic harmonization approach.

Ex.19 - A Minor Pentatonic Scale (Starting Note - C)

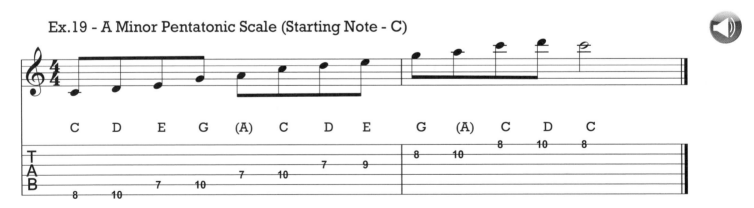

Now that we have two scale positions of A Minor Pentatonic at our disposal, let's attempt to harmonize them verbatim. Before we begin though, I should point out that the following example is going to sound strange and a little out of tune. For now, play and listen to how this example sounds as it is performed (Ex.20).

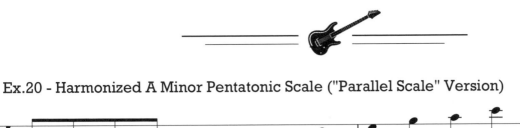

Ex.20 - Harmonized A Minor Pentatonic Scale ("Parallel Scale" Version)

After listening and playing through the previous example, you should be aware of what happens after the initial notes sound together. Examine the notes played together on the and of beat one – 'C' and 'D.' When these two notes are performed together, they produce an interval of a Major 2nd, which is one of the dissonant intervals briefly discussed in the first chapter of this book. You have to admit, this interval sounds bad, doesn't it? To fix this problem, you must arrange the notes differently to avoid note conflicts.

To help you see (and hear) a corrected version of the previous example, play through the next idea for a corrected version (Ex.21).

Ex.21 - Harmonized A Minor Pentatonic (Corrected Version)

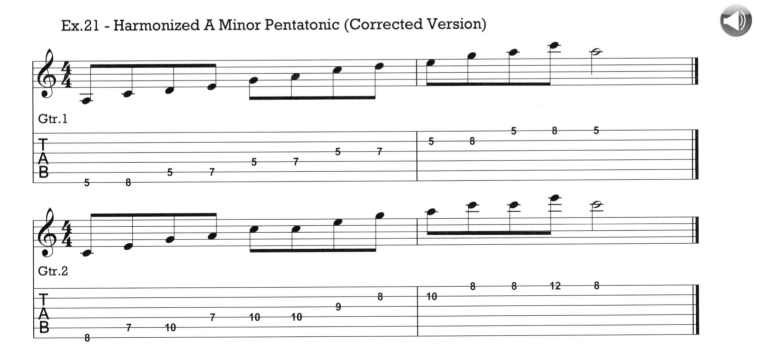

In the previous example (Ex.21), you should examine and notice what was different during the 2nd guitar part when compared Ex.20. Notice that the second guitar bypasses the note D and repeats the note C in the first bar on beat three, and repeats this note again on the and of beat one, and beat two in the second bar. This adjustment remedies the Major 2nd found in Ex.20, and this need for note alteration and adjustment is quite common when writing harmony parts.

To continue with the exploration of Minor Pentatonic scale harmonization, learn the next scale position, revealing the A Minor Pentatonic scale beginning on the note D, a Perfect 4th above the root note A (Ex.22).

Ex.22 - Alternate A Minor Pentatonic Fingering (Starting Note - D)

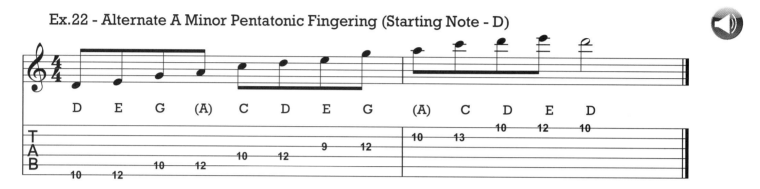

Now that the next scale position of A Minor Pentatonic is comfortable, you can safely harmonize this scale, without the need of altering the harmony notes, as demonstrated in Ex.23.

Ex.23 - Harmonized A Minor Pentatonic (Using 3rds & 4ths)

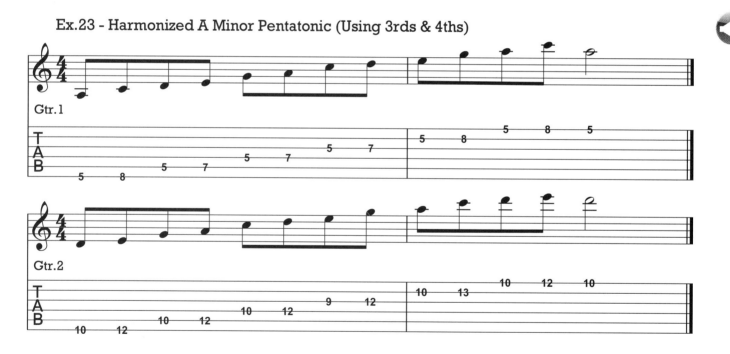

You should notice that the previous example arranges the harmonized notes from two positions of A Minor Pentatonic using a combination of 3rds and 4ths. This strict harmonized scale demonstration aligns the two scale positions together, with no regard to the inclusion of Parallel 4ths. Parallel 4th's are considered wrong in the realm of classical music theory and textbook harmonization technique, but for now, don't worry about these rules, and explore this sound and idea to its fullest. Plenty of guitarists have explored the world of parallel harmonization with reckless abandon, and have produced inspired and legendary sounds in the process.

The next example reveals the next position of A Minor Pentatonic featuring E as the starting note, a Perfect 5th away from the root note A (Ex.24).

Ex.24 - Alternate A Minor Pentatonic Fingering (Starting Note - E)

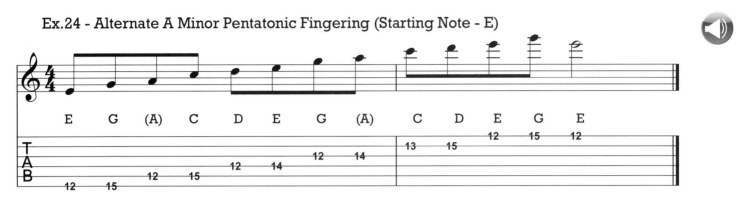

The next phase of applying scale harmonization to the Minor Pentatonic scale features another conflict in classical music theory, the use of Parallel 5ths. For now, don't worry about this standard music "rule" and explore the sound of building harmony using Parallel 5ths (Ex.25).

Ex.25 - Harmonized A Minor Pentatonic Scale (Using Parallel 5ths)

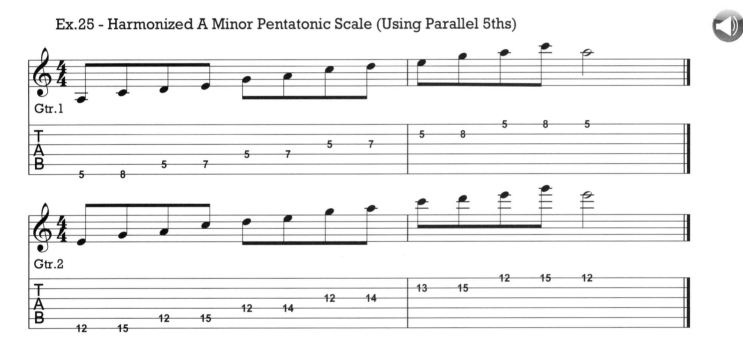

By now, you might be curious about the mention of Parallel 4ths and 5ths in harmonization, and how they are frowned upon in traditional music theory. There rules were established a long time ago, and although the overall sound of strict parallel harmonization in music doesn't sound bad, there are creative ways in which you can substitute intervals when composing harmonized parts, and that will be explained and demonstrated in later section of this book.

The reason these parallel harmonies were demonstrated and used in this portion of the book are for the sake of comparison, and they should be studied to help you understand how harmonization functions in music, and to also help you locate intervallic alternatives that you can choose to use, as your knowledge of building harmonies improves.

Doubling the Minor Pentatonic an octave higher creates Parallel Octaves, which is featured in the next example (Ex.26).

Ex.26 - Harmonized A Minor Pentatonic Scale (Using Parallel Octaves)

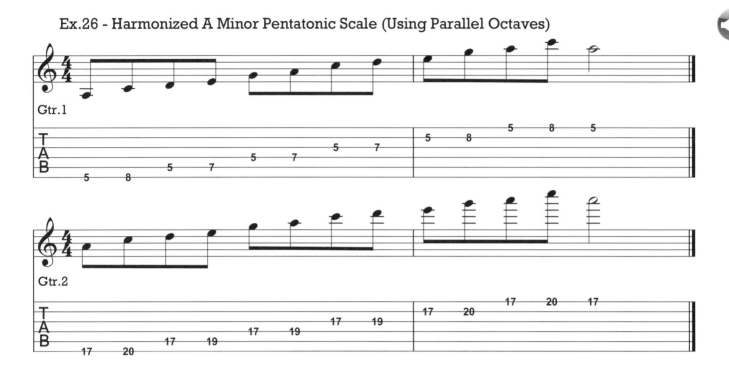

Now that you've worked through a series of parallel harmonization techniques within the confines of traditional Minor Pentatonic scale shapes along the fretboard, you should begin creating phrases and licks from this scale and compare the way various harmonization options sound.

The next example is a basic Minor Pentatonic lick that we'll use to compare a selection of harmonized intervals. Play through Ex.27 and commit it to memory as soon as possible.

Ex.27 - A Minor Pentatonic Lick

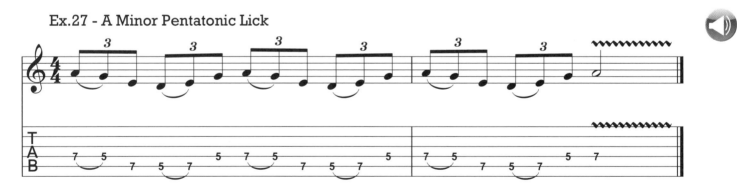

Now that you've learned the foundation lick for the assortment of harmonized ideas we'll create, play through this two-part harmonized version of the lick, where the second guitar is harmonizing using a combination of 2nds and 3rds (Ex.28).

Ex.28 - Harmonized A Minor Pentatonic Lick #1 (Using 2nds & 3rds)

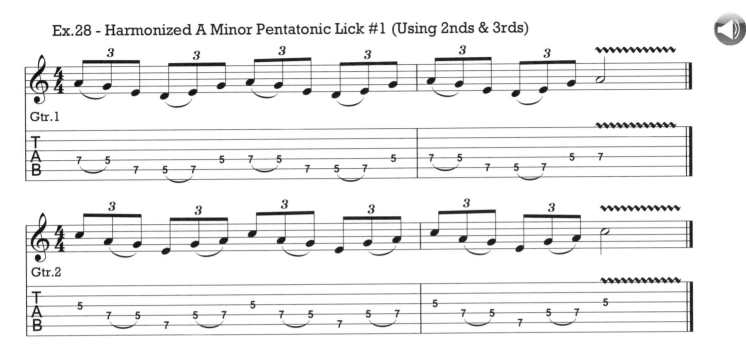

The next example is a basic variation of the previous idea, but now the second guitar is harmonizing using a combination of 2nds, 3rds, and 4ths (Ex.29).

Ex.29 - Harmonized A Minor Pentatonic Lick #2 (Using 2nds, 3rds, & 4ths)

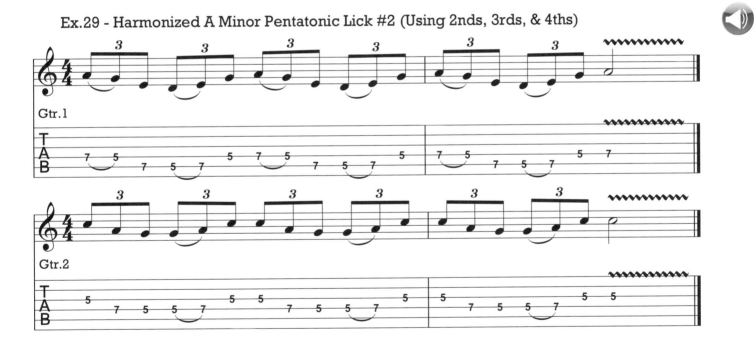

This example features the same idea, but now the second guitar is harmonizing using Parallel 4ths (Ex.30).

Ex.30 - Harmonized A Minor Pentatonic Lick #3 (Using Parallel 4ths)

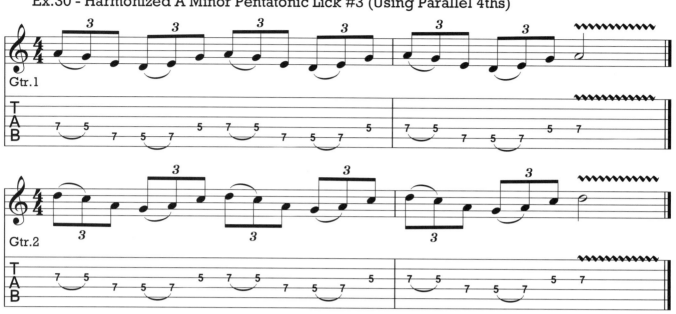

Here's the same idea, now using a Parallel 5th approach (Ex.31).

Ex.31 - Harmonized A Minor Pentatonic Lick #4 (Using Parallel 5ths)

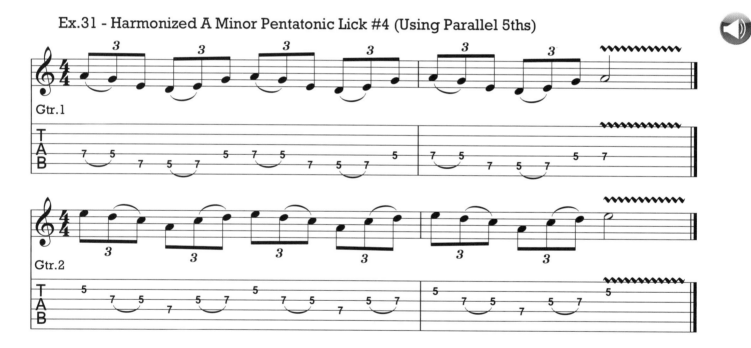

Now that you've explored using Parallel 4ths and 5ths, it is finally time to learn about the harmonization secret weapon. Although parallel 4ths and 5ths don't necessarily sound bad to the ear, the sound they produce seems a little dull, especially compared to the sound of harmonizing and using parallel 3rds and the secret use of harmonizing 6ths.

The interval of Minor and Major 6ths are very important in music, as they create an interesting tonality that creates plenty of interesting directions for chords, melodies, and for use in harmonization. This example features the interval of the 6th, combined with the use of 3rds and 5ths (Ex.32).

Ex.32 - Harmonized A Minor Pentatonic Lick #5 (Using 3rds, 5ths, & 6ths)

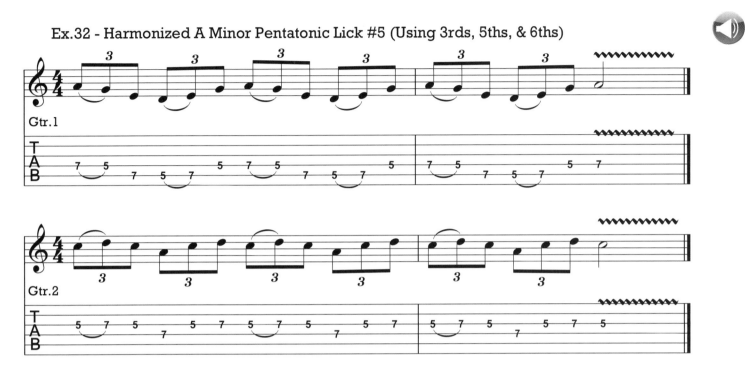

In addition to using 6ths in harmonized phrases and music, you can also explore adding the interval of a 7th to the mix, and their use appears in a variety of musical styles - including blues, jazz, and funk.

Play through the next example, featuring the use of 6ths and 7ths within the confines of a harmonized Minor Pentatonic lick (Ex.33).

Ex.33 - Harmonized A Minor Pentatonic Lick #6 (Using 6ths & 7ths)

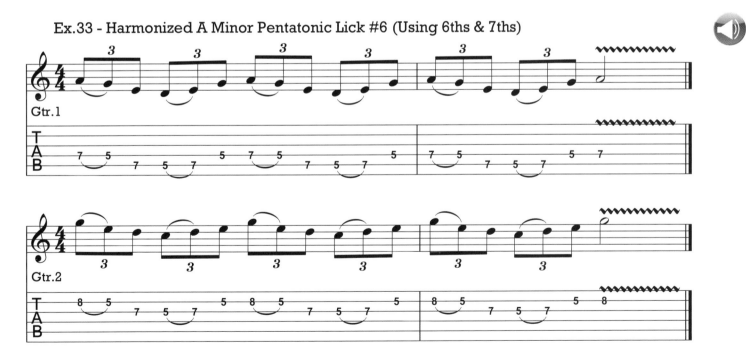

The two previous examples (Ex. 32 & 33) featured the involvement of the 6th and 7th interval within the Minor Pentatonic scale, but if you truly want to explore the sound of harmonizing 6ths, and discover how to use them in harmonized phrases and licks, you'll need to locate the actual interval of a 6th, within whatever key you're working from. Parallel 3rds and 6ths are considered by musical theorists as acceptable, especially when compared to the controversy surrounding the use of Parallel 4ths and 5ths.

To locate Minor and Major 6ths in the key of A, play though the next example (Ex.34).

Ex.34 - Locating the Minor and Major 6ths

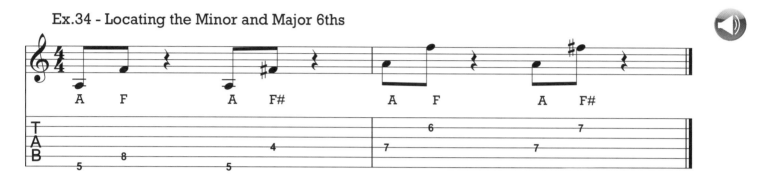

The first bar in the previous example demonstrates the Minor 6th interval (A to F) during beat one, and the Major 6th during beat three in the first bar (A to F#). The second bar shows the same two intervals, written in a higher octave and found within the same fretboard position. Once you are comfortable finding these two important intervals in this position, you should incorporate their sound into the harmonized Minor Pentatonic ideas that were demonstrated in Examples 28-33.

To do this, we'll have to include the note F to the A Minor Pentatonic scale, which might seem out of place, but if you refer to where the Minor Pentatonic scale came from (A Aeolian), you'll find that this note already remains in the key of A Minor, it was simply removed to convert the Natural Minor to the Minor Pentatonic scale.

To continue harmonizing with the use of Parallel 6ths, study the next example carefully, demonstrating a modified Minor Pentatonic fingering performed by Guitar 2 (Ex.35).

Ex.35 - Harmonized A Minor Pentatonic Scale (Using Parallel 6ths)

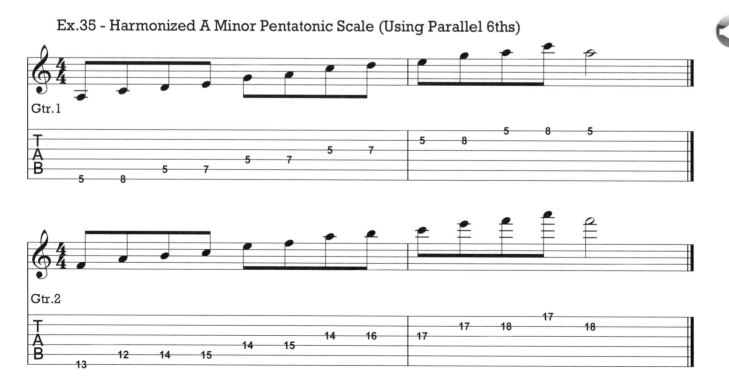

If we apply this modified idea, you'll discover a number of ways to arrange notes and new sounds that you can explore using the 6th interval. This example involves using Parallel 6ths, which help create a very different, yet common sound (Ex.36).

Ex.36 - Harmonized A Minor Pentatonic Lick #7 (Using Parallel 6ths)

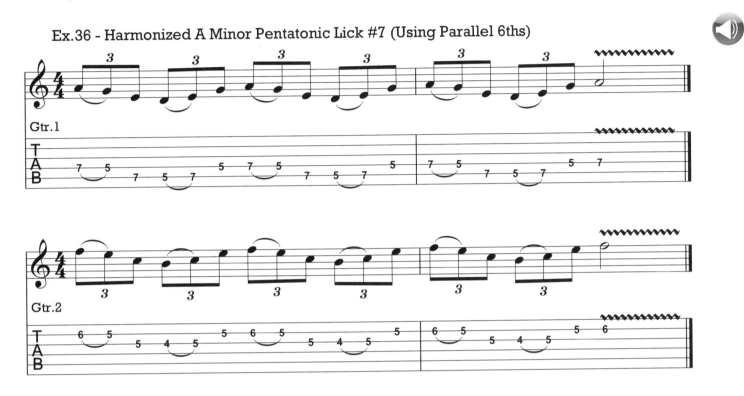

Now that you've discovered how to incorporate Parallel 6ths into harmonized playing, you should strategically arrange the notes so you can perform harmonized ideas using both Parallel 3rds and 6ths. The next example demonstrates this interesting sound, but be sure to watch for the string-skipping found during the second guitar part, which allows for this intervallic movement to occur (Ex.37).

Ex.37 - Harmonized A Minor Pentatonic Lick #8 (Using Parallel 3rds & 6ths)

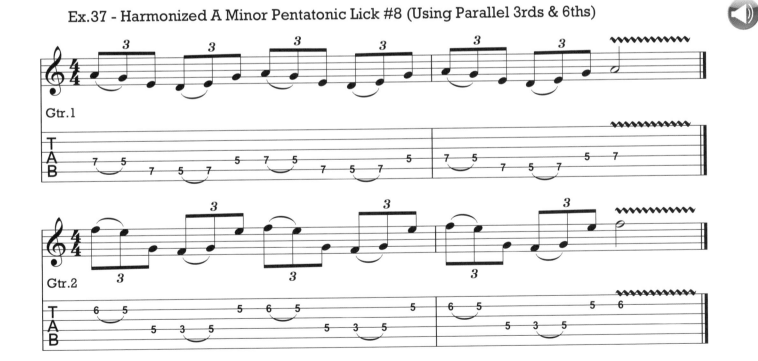

The next example features the use of Parallel Octaves into this steam of harmonized ideas, creating an entirely new harmonized flavor and sound (Ex.38).

Ex.38 - Harmonized A Minor Pentatonic Lick #9 (Using Parallel Octaves)

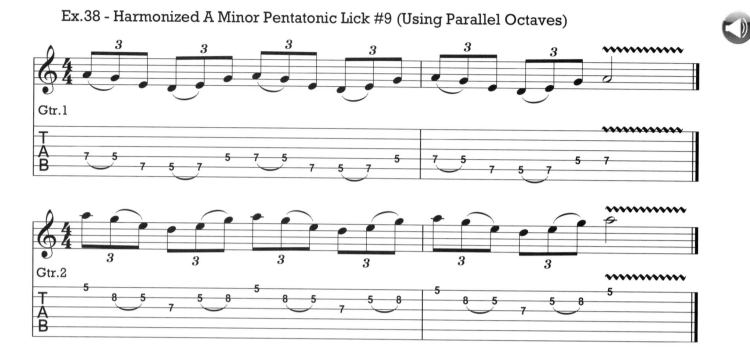

This example borrows the pattern of notes the harmony guitar was performing in the previous example (Gtr.2), so be sure to play through it to become more comfortable with the phrase before moving to the next group of harmonized ideas (Ex.39).

Ex.39 - A Minor Pentatonic Lick

Now that we have a new lick to harmonize and a fresh sound for the ears, we can begin experimenting with some different harmonized approaches and ideas on the fretboard, similar to what was demonstrated with Ex.27-38.

Chord progressions dictate everything in music From the scales and notes that can be used during a melody or fill, to the arrangement of notes during a guitar solo or harmonized section, the sooner you understand the importance of the chords and chord progression that you're playing over, the better. Knowing what you can play within the confines of a chord progression during any piece of music, is paramount in becoming an aware and knowledgeable musician.

The next example demonstrates taking the idea from Ex.39, but now we've added the 6th (the note F) to the A Minor Pentatonic phrase (Ex.40).

Ex.40 - Harmonized A Minor Pentatonic Lick #10 (Gtr.2 Target Note - F)

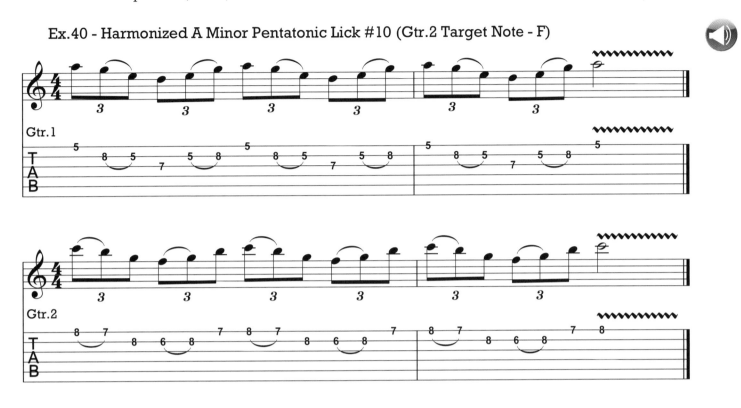

To begin understanding the 6th and why we might manipulate it, let's say that you're playing over a Am – D9 chord progression. This chord progression dictates what you can play or target within your musical phrases and licks. The note F# is found within the D9 chord, and whenever that chord appears, you should target F# instead of F natural, which will create an A Dorian mode tonality.

The next example reveals this situation on a silver platter. As you examine what is going on here, you should notice that this is the exact same phrase, but the note F has been replaced with the note F# (Ex.41).

Ex.41 - Harmonized A Minor Pentatonic Lick #11 (Gtr.2 Target Note - F#)

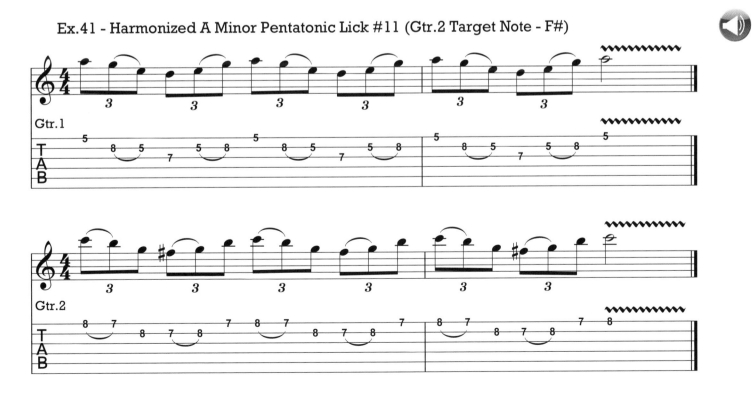

This example features playing the harmony guitar line one octave below the melody (Ex.42).

Ex.42 - Harmonized A Minor Pentatonic Lick #12 (Harmony 1 Octave Below)

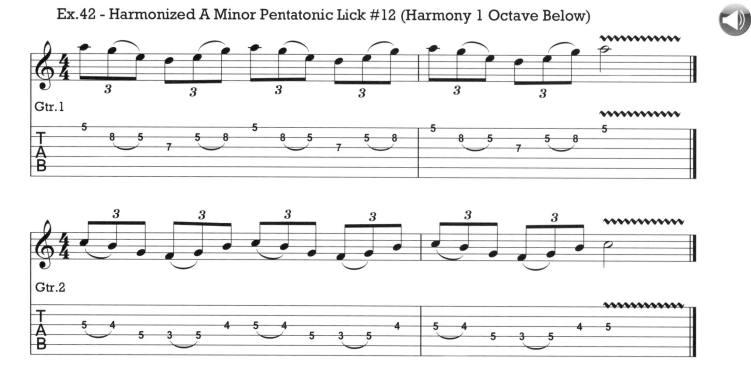

This example features the same idea, but now we're performing the harmony part two-octaves below the melody (Ex.43).

Ex.43 - Harmonized A Minor Pentatonic Lick #13 (Harmony 2 Octaves Below)

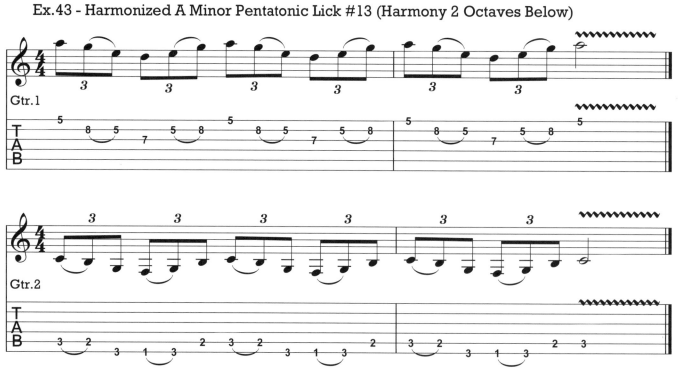

Here's another glimpse into arranging above and below the melody, featuring harmonizing this lick using Parallel 4ths above the melody (Ex.44).

Ex.44 - Harmonized A Minor Pentatonic Lick #14 (Using Parallel 4ths Above)

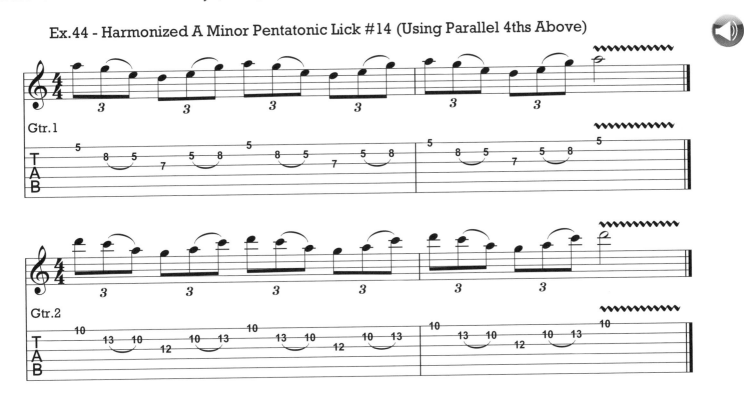

This is the same idea, only now the harmony part is played a Parallel 4ths below the melody, creating an entirely different harmonized sound (Ex.45).

Ex.45 - Harmonized A Minor Pentatonic Lick #15 (Using Parallel 4ths Below)

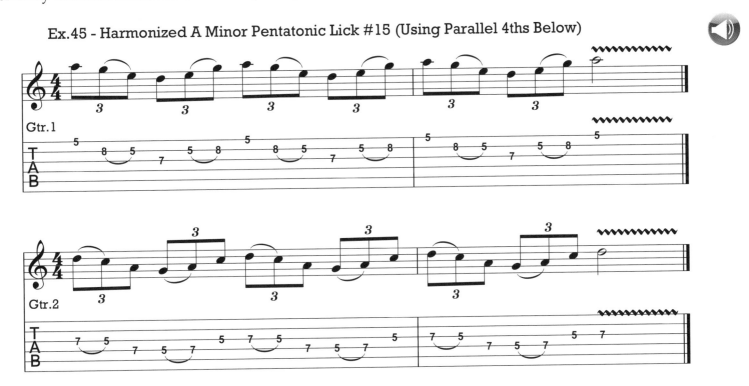

The next example demonstrates the same phrase using Parallel 5ths above the melody (Ex.46).

Ex.46 - Harmonized A Minor Pentatonic Lick #16 (Using Parallel 5ths Above)

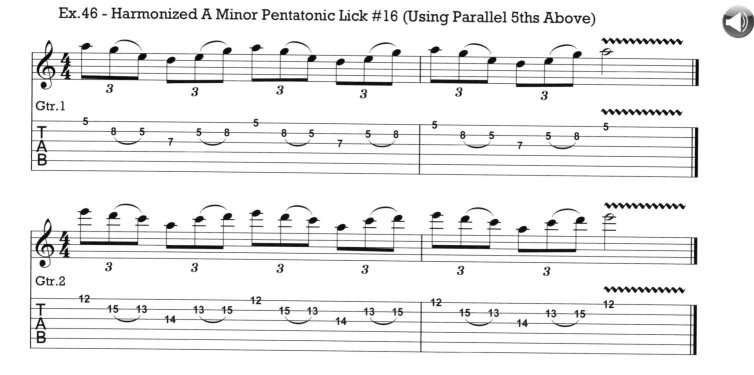

This variation features the same concept, but the harmony is played a Parallel 5ths below the melody (Ex.47).

Ex.47 - Harmonized A Minor Pentatonic Lick #17 (Using Parallel 5ths Below)

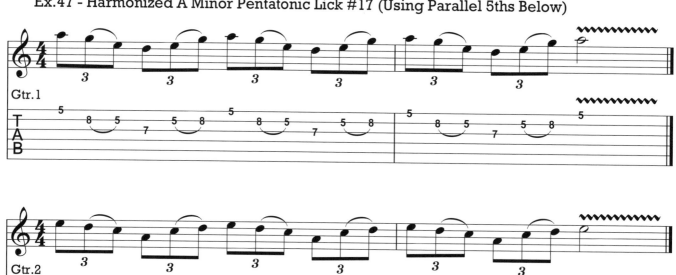

Here's another idea to take these harmony parts even further, featuring the use of 6ths and 7ths in the harmony, placed above the melody (Ex.48).

Ex.48 - Harmonized A Minor Pentatonic Lick #18 (Using 6ths & 7ths Above)

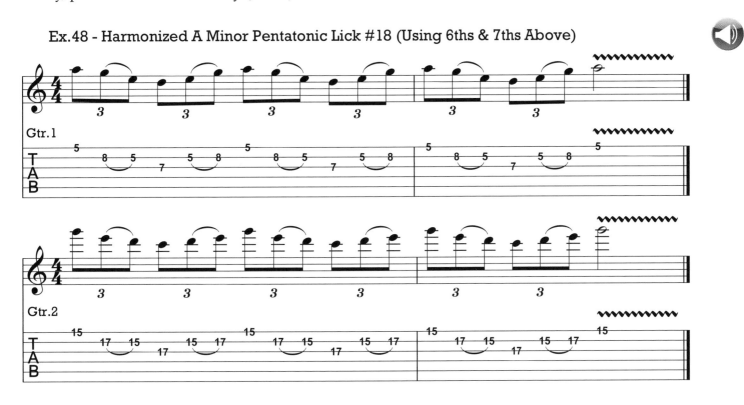

Now try the same idea using Parallel Octaves above the melody line (Ex.49).

Ex.49 - Harmonized A Minor Pentatonic Lick #19 (Using Parallel Octave Above)

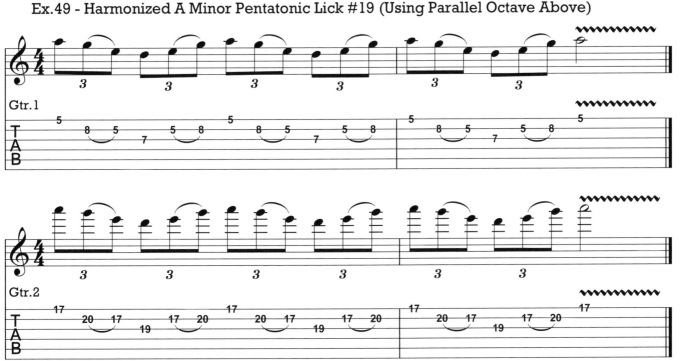

To take things even further and create a range of interesting sounds, the next example features an ascending harmony part, harmonized with a stationary melody part (Ex.50).

Ex.50 - Harmonized A Minor Pentatonic Lick #20 (Ascending Harmony Variation)

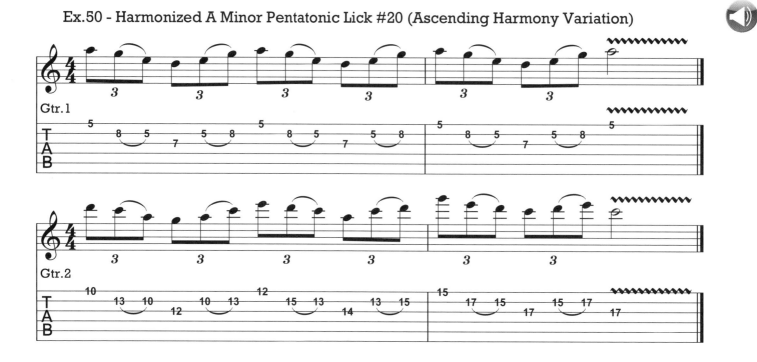

This example creates a more advanced of the previous example (Ex.50), creating a simultaneous ascending melody and harmony idea that moves up the fretboard simultaneously (Ex.51).

Ex.51 - Harmonized A Minor Pentatonic Lick #21 (Dual Ascending Variation)

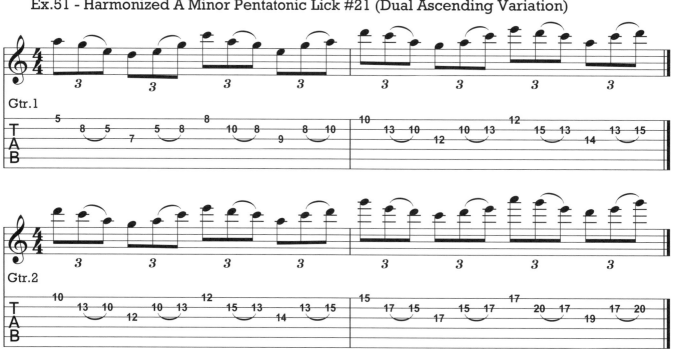

Chapter 3 – Two-Part Harmony Using Major Scales

Now that we've explored two-part harmonization techniques centered around Minor keys and scales, you should explore harmonizing Major keys and scales, and you should become aware of relative keys. For every Minor or Major key, there is a relative key that contain the exact same notes, yet they yield very different results.

For example, the notes found in the A Natural Minor scale are the exact same notes found in the C Major scale, but the only difference is the emphasis of the individual notes as they're played over an appropriate chord or within the key. When you're playing in the key of A Minor, the note A is functioning as the root and given the strongest emphasis. When you are in the key of C Major, the note C is functioning as the root and given the strongest emphasis.

To further understand the concept of relative Major and Minor keys, play thorough the next example, which compares the notes from A Minor and C Major side-by-side (Ex.52).

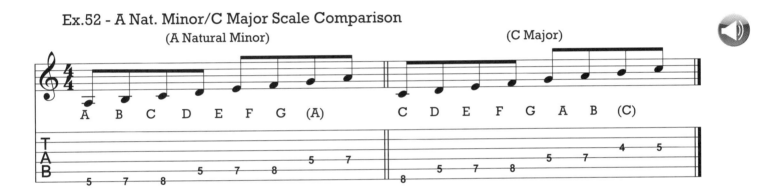

If you compare the notes from these two keys, you should notice the exact same notes, only in a different order. The noticeable difference is where they begin and end, and the overall mood of how they sound when they are played over the appropriate chord. A Minor has a dark sound, as Minor keys/chords/scales sound sad, while C Major sounds bright, as Major keys/chords/scales sound happy.

The harmonization of Major scales (including the Major Pentatonic scale), is quite common in most forms of music. Although it's rare to hear hard rock or metal music written in a Major key, the use of Major keys in rock, especially country and Southern rock, is very common. Think of Lynryd Skynyrd or the Allman Brothers Band when exploring this style of harmonization.

Once you have some Major key ideas under your fingers and in your head, you're ready to begin exploring the realm of harmonizing Major keys. To tap into your first Major scale harmonization idea, you should learn this alternate fingering for the C Major scale (Ex.53).

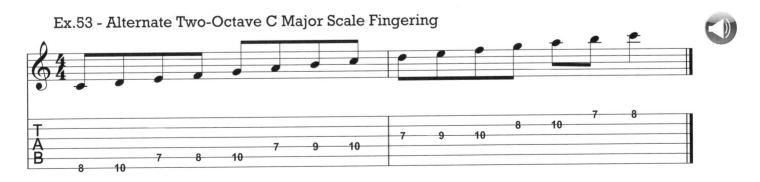

Now that you have a new scale sound and fingering under your fingers, play through the next example, featuring a harmonized C Major scale using Parallel 3rds above (Ex.54).

Ex.54 Harmonized C Major Scale (Using Parallel 3rd Above)

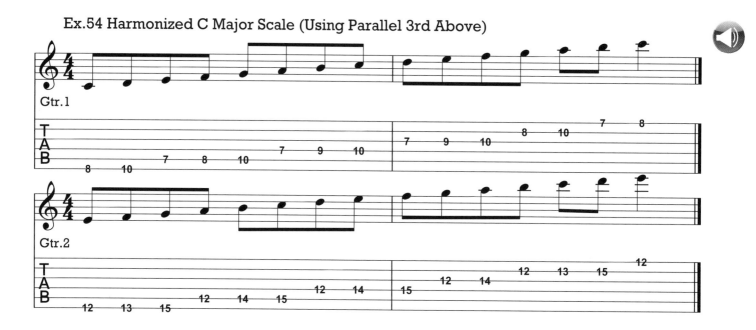

In this example, you should notice that the scale position and fingering played during the second guitar part (the harmony part), is the exact same scale fingering you learned in Ex.14 from the first chapter of this book. If you're confused about how this recycling of a scale was possible, study the notes Gtr.2 is playing in this example and notice that while the pattern of notes remain the same, the emphasis on the notes in the melody have changed from A (creating a Minor sound), to C (creating a Major sound), which allow the harmony guitar line to reuse the same scale fingering we've already learned.

If this harmonized idea were played over an A Minor chord, the tonality would be in a Minor key and sound produced would be the A Minor scale. On the other hand, if this example was played over a C Major chord, this harmonized idea would sound like the C Major scale.

For another look at this idea, play through a harmonized C Major scale with the harmony line playing a Parallel 6th below (Ex.55).

Ex.55 Harmonized C Major Scale (Using Parallel 6th Below)

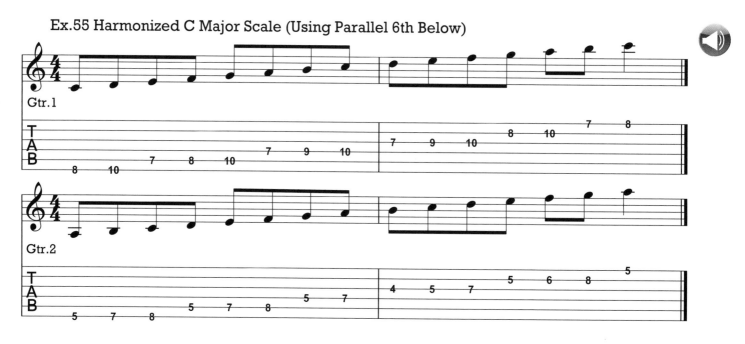

From here, you should harmonize the C Major scale using other interval distances (such as 4ths and 5ths), which will help you become comfortable with new sounds, concepts, and ideas. To help you continue with this study and Major key licks, phrases, and ideas, the next example reveals the C Major Pentatonic scale, a very common scale found in a variety of musical styles (Ex.56).

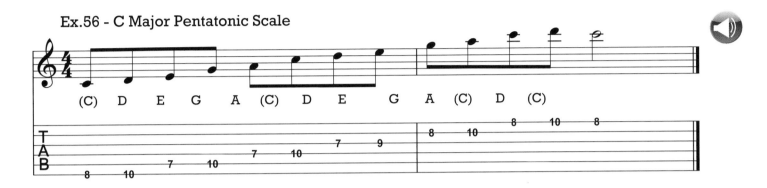

Once again, you should notice that we're using the same notes from the A Minor Pentatonic scale in the previous example (Ex.57), only the emphasis has shifted from A to C, creating a Major Pentatonic sound.

This example features harmonizing the C Major scale using a combination of 3rds, 4ths, and 5ths (Ex.58).

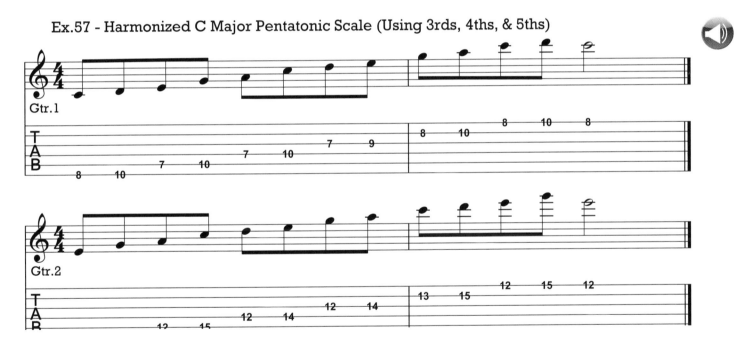

To transform the previous idea and allow the use of Parallel 6ths, the next example features a relocated C Major scale position in the harmony part (Gtr.2). Notice that the starting note of the second guitar begins on the note F, a 6th above the starting note C in the melody (Ex.58).

Ex.58 Harmonized C Major Pentatonic Scale (Using Parallel 6ths)

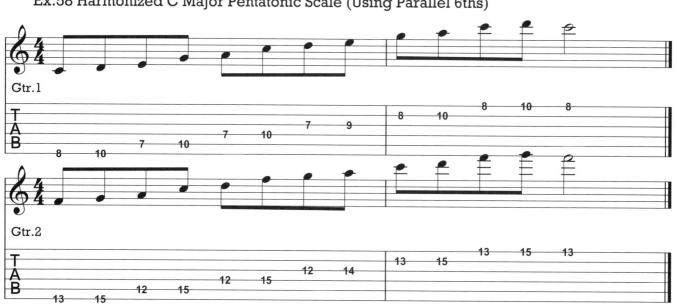

To really help you get a grip on harmonizing Major Pentatonic ideas, play through the next example featuring a basic Major Pentatonic lick that we'll use as a guide for a variety of harmonized approaches, similar to what was shown and discussed in the the previous chapter. To begin working through Major keys, start by learning this simple starting phrase, which will serve as the melody (Ex.59).

Ex.59 C Major Pentatonic Lick

Now that you have the melody lick in your head, play through the next example using harmonized Parallel 3rd and 4ths above the melody (Ex.60).

Ex.60 Harmonized C Major Pentatonic Lick #1 (Using Parallel 3rd & 4ths Above)

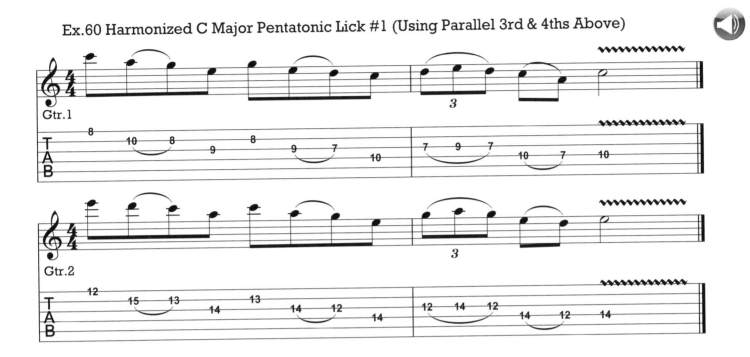

The next example is a variation of the previous idea, and features harmonizing the Major Pentatonic lick using Parallel 4ths and 5ths below (Ex.61).

Ex.61 Harmonized C Major Pentatonic Lick #2 (Using Parallel 4ths & 5ths Above)

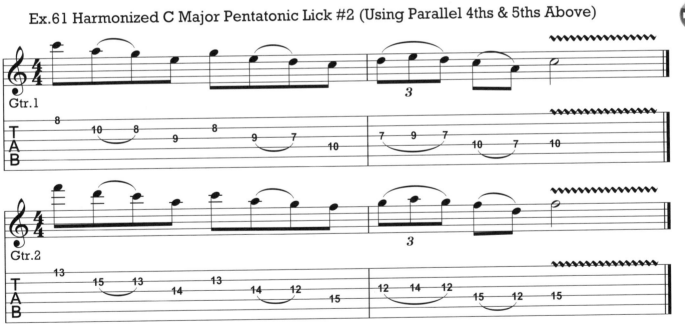

Here's another variation, this time showcasing a harmonized version of this lick using Parallel 6ths above (Ex.62).

Ex.62 Harmonized C Major Pentatonic Lick #3 (Using Parallel 6ths Above)

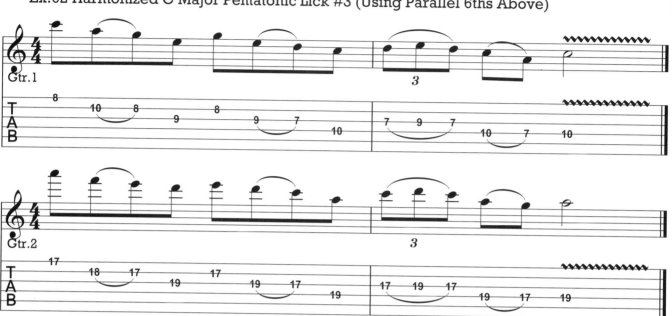

Studying and analyzing harmonized guitar parts from popular songs will help you gain more insight into how to go about creating your own harmonized ideas. The knowledge and inspiration you'll gain by learning songs that you're familiar with will push your harmonized ideas further.

Bob Weir

Chapter 4 – Harmonized String Bending

String bending on the guitar is a common technique that guitarists use in every style of music (except for classical guitarists), and for many guitarists, the individual bending style and overall approach when bending strings defines them as a player.

When harmonizing two guitar parts and incorporating the string bending technique, the subtle differences in the parts can lead to some interesting sounds and inspired results. From the slight changes in pitch and inclusion of slight bending and vibrato movements, to creating separate parts that move together using different intervallic approaches, these variations in pitch and technique can create expressive and unique harmonized music moments.

To begin using this technique in harmonized part writing and performance, you must be aware that if the harmonized parts are incorporating string bending techniques together, both of the parts being harmonized must be played efficiently and in tune. Otherwise the harmonized result will sound out-of-tune and quite strange to the ear. Bending to pitch and the accuracy of bent situations in music is crucial when using this technique with one guitar, but the importance of being aware of the actual pitches being sounded and performed when harmonizing two (or more) guitars together, cannot be overstated or ignored.

The first example in this chapter features a basic bending lick in the key of D Minor, and uses the D Minor Pentatonic scale for its selection of notes (Ex.63).

Ex.63 - D Minor Pentatonic Bending Lick

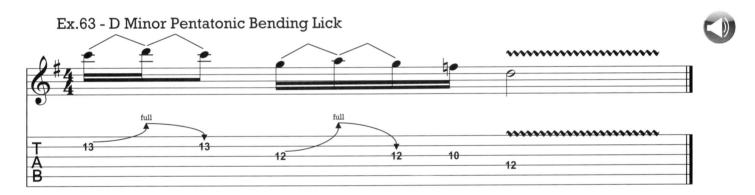

As you practice this bending lick, pay attention to the actual pitch of the strings and the notes that you're bending from and toward as the string bends are applied. Before we attempt to harmonize this lick, you must be certain that the two string bend occurrences during this lick are accurate. The note performed at the start of this example C, must be bent accurately a whole-step (two-frets on the guitar) higher, to the note D, and then this note is returned to the starting pitch C, during the release of the bend. The bent note that occurs during beat two, the note G, must sound a whole-step higher, reaching the note A perfectly, before returning the bent note back to its starting pitch, the note G.

Practice this lick a few more times and play along with the audio demonstration, to make sure that you're accurately executing this lick, before moving ahead in this chapter and exploring additional harmonized string bend approaches.

Now that you're comfortable accurately performing the string bend found in the previous example, you should be ready to harmonize this phrase, a number of different ways. To begin, practice harmonizing this bending lick using Parallel 3rds above (Ex.64).

Ex.64 - Harmonized D Minor Pentatonic Bending Lick (Using Parallel 3rds)

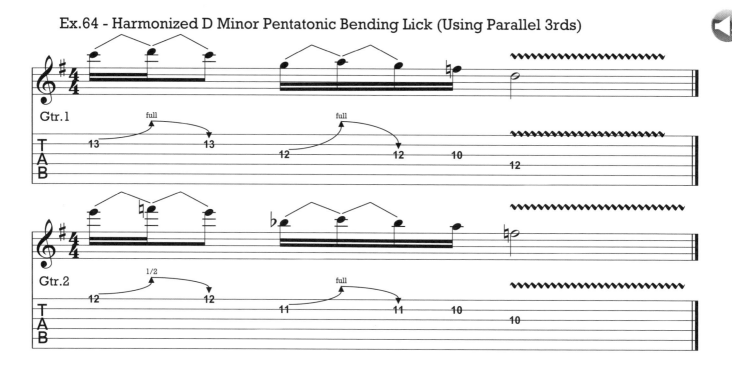

Next try the same idea, but this time the harmony part is playing and bending strings a Parallel 6ths above (Ex.65).

Ex.65 - Harmonized D Minor Pentatonic Bending Lick (Using Parallel 3rds)

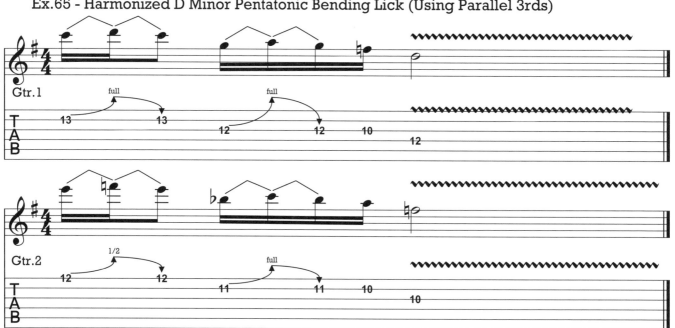

In the previous example, notice that the harmony guitar (Gtr.2) is performing half-step bends to accommodate the Parallel 6ths, and the final note is bent upward. On the other hand, the melody part frets the last note, which creates a slight variation to the end of this idea.

The next variation of this harmonized lick involves the harmony part performing string bends an octave below the melody. As you play through this example, you should immediately notice the difference in the overall sound, partially due to the inclusion of Parallel Octaves and the fact the harmony part features string bending on wound strings, creating a big difference in the tonal character of this idea (Ex.66).

Ex.66 - Harmonized D Minor Pentatonic Bending Lick (Using Parallel Octaves)

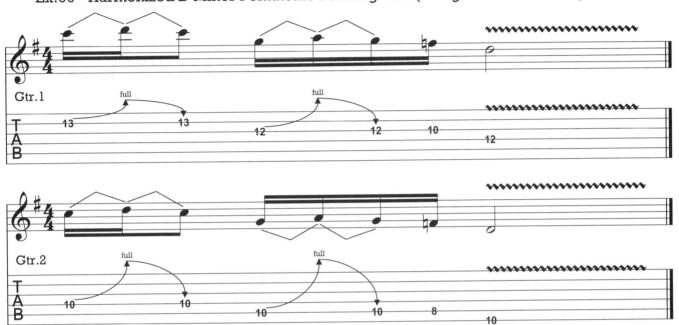

Brad Whitford

Chapter 5 – Three and Four-Part Harmonization

The final chapter in this book will discuss and examine arranging harmonized guitar parts using three and four-part harmony. Arranging for three and four-part harmony is more complicated when compared to the two-part harmonization technique we've already explored. As you continue to locate and discover different ways of arranging parts for two guitars playing in harmony, the options available to you when arranging three and four-part harmony becomes more refined and strict. Just as we found when arranging parts for two guitars, when you have three or four parts that are simultaneously harmonized, you have to pay considerable attention to the notes and intervals being performed, and even closer attention to the underlying chord progression, for things arranged in this manner to sound right.

The basis for creating three-part harmony ideas centers on the concept of harmonizing triads within the three guitar parts playing together. Triads are the three notes that construct basic Major and Minor chords or arpeggios.

To begin this area of the book, let's shift to a different key, to freshen the ears and give the fingers a new key to explore. The key of E Minor contains the notes E-F#-G-A-B-C-D-E. If we were to take the first, third, and fifth notes from this scale and play them together as a chord or separately as an arpeggio, you would discover a basic E Minor triad.

The next example features a basic E Minor triad based around open position on the guitar (Ex.67).

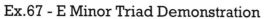

Ex.67 - E Minor Triad Demonstration

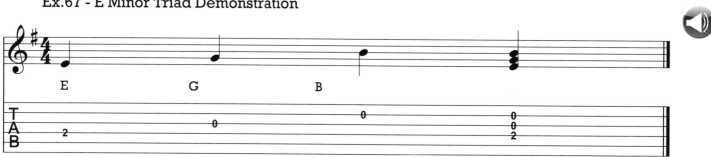

In the previous example, you should notice during the first three beats, the separated notes E-G-B create a basic E Minor triad arpeggio when they're strummed together as a chord on beat four. As soon as you understand what triads are and how you can use them to build powerful sounding three-part harmonies, the sooner you'll be on your way to creating different types of interesting harmonized ideas for multiple guitars.

The next example demonstrates taking the E Minor triad shown in the previous example, and relocates this series of three notes into a different octave, expanding where and how you can perform this triad on the guitar (Ex.68).

Ex.68 - Triads in E Minor

(E Minor Triad = Root - m3rd - P5th)

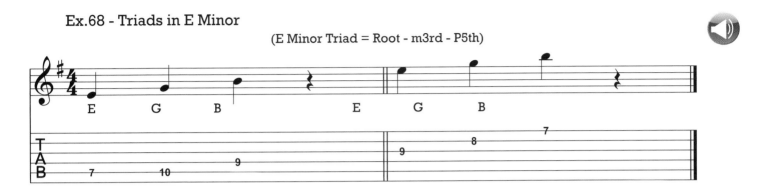

Now that you're comfortable relocating these three notes to another fretboard location, learn how to play the E Natural Minor scale in this position of the neck (Ex.69).

Ex.69 - One Octave E Natural Minor Scale

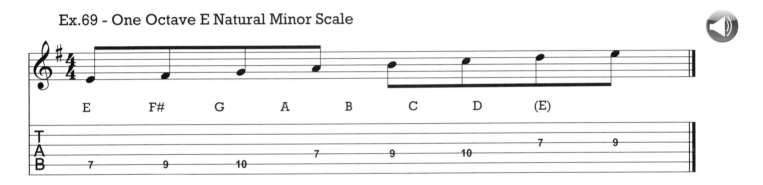

Once you have the basis for where we're going to harmonize this scale to create three-part harmony, you should begin with the two-part harmonized version of this scale (Ex.70).

Ex.70 - Harmonized E Nat. Minor Scale (Using Two-Part Harmony)

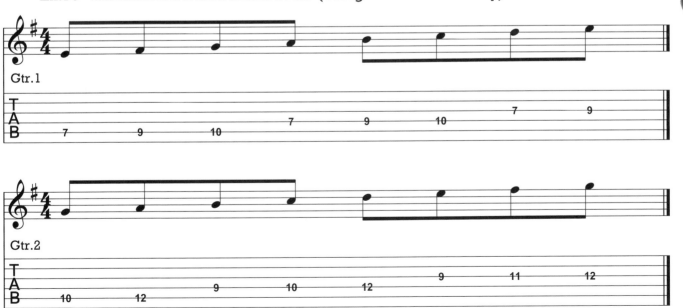

The next example demonstrates the E Natural Minor scale harmonized in three parts, and creates a full and interesting sound. If you carefully examine the starting note of each part of this idea, notice that each of the three guitar parts begin from each of the three notes found in the E Minor triad (E-G-B), creating a basic three-part harmonized E Minor scale demonstration.

Ex.71 - Harmonized E Nat. Minor Scale (Using Three-Part Harmony)

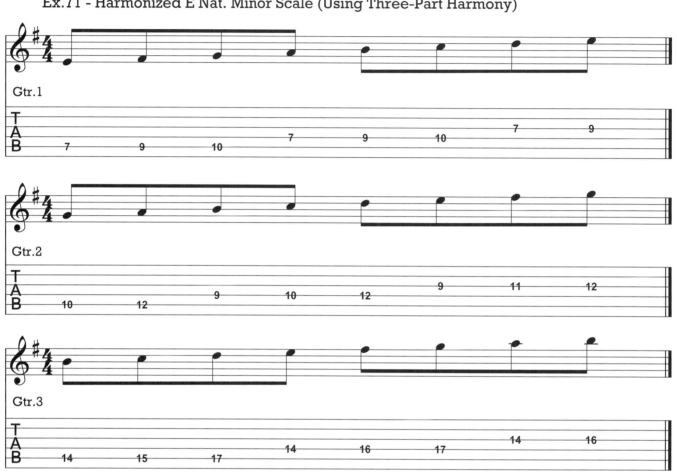

Now that you've adapted the sound of three-part harmonies using a Minor key, you should transform what was demonstrated to a Major key. To keep things simple, let's use the Relative Major of E Minor - G Major. The key of G Major features the exact same notes when compared to E Minor, but now the emphasis is on the note G, instead of the note E.

To begin, locate the G Major triad, which contains the notes G-B-D - the root, third, and fifth of this chord (Ex.72).

Ex.72 - Triads in G Major

The next step is locating how and where to perform a G Major scale (Ex.73).

Ex.73 - One Octave G Major Scale

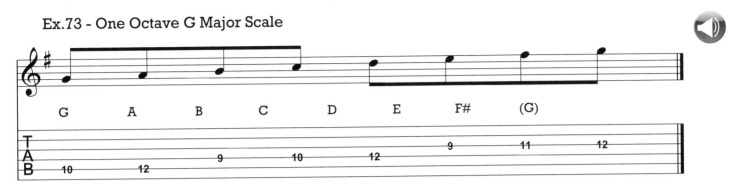

Now that you've found the triad and the scale that match the key of G Major, perform this scale using two-part harmony in Ex.74.

Ex.74 - Harmonized G Major Scale (Using Two-Part Harmony)

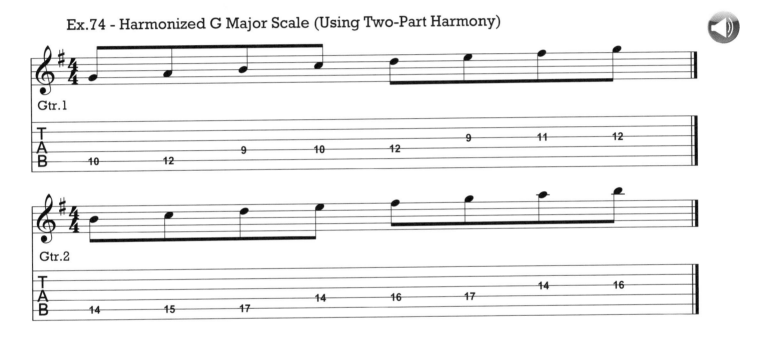

The next step in creating three-part harmonization in G Major is the same as what was demonstrated and discussed for creating the three-part harmony of the E Minor scale (Ex.75). Once you have the two-part harmonized version of G Major under your belt, you can add the third guitar part, creating a three-part harmonized version of the G Major scale (Ex.76).

Ex.76 - Harmonized G Major Scale (Using Four-Part Harmony)

Building three-part harmony guitar parts can take some time understanding and getting used to when compared to building and arranging two-part guitar harmonies. This is due to the fact that there are three independently functions parts performing simultaneously. This added harmony part, can complicate note conflicts and strange harmonies can develop if you're not aware of exactly what is being arranged and performed together. Correcting and adjusting note or interval conflicts must be applied to create three-part harmonies that will sound right to the ear.

As discussed earlier in this book, it's highly recommended to experiment with recording yourself or playing harmonized parts with two other guitarists to expand your horizons and continue becoming comfortable with arranging harmonized guitar parts. Give yourself time getting used to arranging harmonies in three-parts, continue to experiment with these sounds and ideas, and continue your quest for building a wall of three-part harmonies.

Now that you've tapped into developing and arranging three-part harmonies, you should briefly learn the basics of arranging four-part harmonies to expand your arrangement options and create an even bigger sound.

Arranging four-part harmonies is similar to what was discussed previously in this chapter, but now another part has been added, which increases the difficultly level when creating this type of harmony.

The easiest method of creating a four-part harmony, would be taking what was shown in the previous example (Ex.76), and adding another part at the bottom of the harmonized parts. In this case, we're going to add a part to the bottom of this demonstration (Gtr.4), which is adding an additional part one octave lower than the melody part performed by Guitar 1 (Ex.77).

Ex.77 - 'My Country Tis Of The' - Melody Using Four-Part Harmony

Once you're comfortable creating four-part harmony, you can experiment with allowing the fourth part to introduce different intervals to these ideas (such as 4ths, 5ths, or 6ths), which will help you create some interesting and unusual sounds when using four-part harmonization.

Harmonized Suggested Listening

Allman Brothers Band
'Jessica'
'Revival'
'Ramblin' Man'

The Beatles
'And Your Bird Can Sing'

Boston
'More Than A Feeling'
'Piece of Mind'

Derek and the Dominoes
'Layla'

The Eagles
'Hotel California'

Peter Frampton
'Do You Feel Like I Do'

Iron Maiden
'Aces High'
'The Trooper'

Kiss
'Detroit Rock City'

Lenny Kravitz
'Are You Gonna Go My Way'

Led Zeppelin
'Black Dog'
'Ramble On'

Yngwie Malmsteen
'Black Star'

Megadeth
'Hangar 18'
'Peace Sells (But Who's Buying)'

Metallica
'Master of Puppets'
'Orion'

Molly Hatchet
'Flirtin' With Disaster'

Queen
'Keep Yourself Alive'
'Killer Queen'
'God Save The Queen'

Queensryche
'I Don't Believe In Love'

Racer X
'Scit Scat Wah'
'Technical Difficulties'

Joe Satriani
'Hill Of The Skull'
'Crushing Day'

Scorpions
'No One Like You'
'Rock You Like A Hurricane'

Steely Dan
'Reelin' In The Years'

Tesla
'Modern Day Cowboy'

Thin Lizzy
'Cowboy Song'
'The Boys Are Back In Town'

Steve Vai
'The Attitude Song'

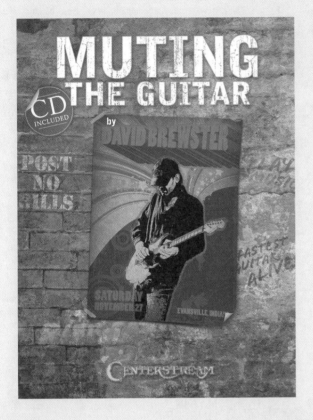
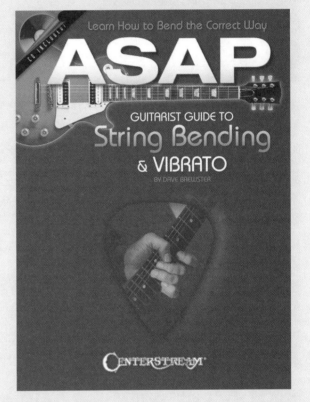

More Great Guitar Books from Centerstream...

SCALES & MODES IN THE BEGINNING
by Ron Middlebrook

INCLUDES TAB

The most comprehensive and complete scale book written especially for the guitar. Chapers include: Fretboard Visualization • Scale Terminology • Scales and Modes • and a Scale to Chord Guide.
00000010...$11.95

FINGERSTYLE GUITAR
by Ken Perlman

INCLUDES TAB

Teaches beginning or advanced guitarists how to master the basic musical skills of fingerpicking techniques needed to play folk, blues, fiddle tunes or ragtime on guitar.
00000081 Book Only....................................$24.95

POWER RHYTHM GUITAR
by Ron Middlebrook
with Dave Celentano

This book/CD pack features 31 lessons for rhythm guitar that you can play by yourself, in a band, or as a back-up musician. Includes full band examples in many musical styles, including basic rock, country, hard rock, heavy metal, reggae, blues, funk, and more.
00000113 Book/CD Pack........................$19.95

THE FLATPICKER'S GUIDE
by Dan Crary

INCLUDES TAB

This instruction/method book for flatpicking teaches how to play accompaniments, cross-picking, and how to play lick strums. Examples in the book are explained on the accompanying CD. The CD also allows the player to play along with the songs in the book.
00000231 Book/CD Pack............................$19.95

ACOUSTIC BLUES GUITAR
by Kenny Sultan

INCLUDES TAB DVD

This book/CD pack for intermediate-level players incorporates slide or bottleneck playing in both open and standard tunings. All songs are primarily fingerstyle with a monotone bass used for most.
00000157 Book/CD Pack..........................$18.95
00000336 DVD $19.95

GUITAR CHORDS PLUS
by Ron Middlebrook

INCLUDES TAB

A comprehensive study of normal and extended chords, tuning, keys, transposing, capo use, and more. Includes over 500 helpful photos and diagrams, a key to guitar symbols, and a glossary of guitar terms.
00000011..$11.95

BLUES GUITAR
by Kenny Sultan

INCLUDES TAB

Through instructional text and actual songs, the author covers blues in five different keys and positions. Covers fingerstyle blues, specific techniques, open tuning, and bottleneck guitar. The CD includes all songs and examples, most played at slow speed and at regular tempo.
00000283 Book/CD Pack..........................$17.95

ARRANGING FOR OPEN GUITAR TUNINGS
By Dorian Michael

INCLUDES TAB DVD

This book/CD pack teaches intermediate-level guitarists how to choose an appropriate tuning for a song, develop an arrangement, and solve any problems that may arise while turning a melody into a guitar piece to play and enjoy.
00000313 Book/CD Pack $19.95

BLUES GUITAR LEGENDS
by Kenny Sultan

INCLUDES TAB DVD

This book/CD pack allows you to explore the styles of Lightnin' Hopkins, Blind Blake, Mississippi John Hurt, Blind Boy Fuller, and Big Bill Broonzy. Through Sultan's arrangements, you will learn how studying the masters can help you develop your own style.
00000181 Book/CD Pack..........................$19.95
00000193 DVD $19.95

FLYING FINGERS
by Dave Celentano

INCLUDES TAB

This book/CD pack offers clear demos of techniques proven to increase speed, precision and dexterity. 32 examples cover arpeggios, different picking techniques, melodic sequences, and more. The CD demonstrates each technique at three speeds: slow, medium and fast.
00000103 Book/CD Pack..........................$15.95

CENTERSTREAM®

P.O. Box 17878 - Anaheim Hills, CA 92817
(714) 779-9390   www.centerstream-usa.com